© Parham Donyai 2024

All rights reserved. No part of this book may be reproduced, stored in a retrieval system, or transmitted in any form or by any means, electronic, mechanical, photocopying, recording, or otherwise, without the prior written permission of the publisher.

Published by: Active Press

For more information, please visit:
www.parhamdonyai.com

Dedicated to all those who suffer, openly or in silence. To those who are unable to get what they want, keep what they get or live the life they crave for and deserve. Let's change all that.

PROLOGUE

Since the dawn of time, countless psychological principles have emerged, each promising to broaden the mind and help us reach our goals. Through scientific advancements, these principles have evolved, becoming either simpler or more complex. There is no single right or wrong approach; no universal solution fits everyone perfectly.

Is there a common ground that unites all experts in the field of human growth and potential? Probably not!

Enter "The Secret Human Operating System" (SHOS), a groundbreaking concept that suggests we are primarily driven by a unique internal Operating System. Each person's SHOS is distinct, and it can evolve over time. In this book, you will find a comprehensive list of the main Human Operating Systems and detailed instructions on how to identify your own.

Unlocking your SHOS is the key to immense personal growth and the achievement of your goals. This discovery requires effort and dedication, and while the journey may be challenging, it is profoundly rewarding.

Once you uncover your SHOS, you will see the world through a new lens, empowering you to transform yourself, your life, and your destiny. Moreover, understanding others' SHOS will enable you to forge more effective and meaningful relationships.

Your incredible journey of self-discovery and transformation is about to begin. Good luck, and welcome to a new era of personal potential!

1. WHAT IS THE SECRET HUMAN OPERATING SYSTEM?

The Secret Human Operating System (SHOS) is at the centre of who you are. It dictates your being, why you do the things you do, what drives you, what holds you back, why you make decisions as you do, how you make decisions, what you think of yourself, your inner self-talk, how you interact with others, how you react to situations and every other aspect of your life.

The Secret Human Operating System is actually not that secret. It is there in plain sight for most of your life, however you need to know what to look for and how to look for it. Bear in mind, your SHOS can change over time.

The phrase "most of your life" may be confusing. After all, if you are running some sort of secret operating system within you, surely it should be there all your life? From birth?

The answer is a bit more complex. Yes, most people start to run on some sort of Operating System once they begin learning to speak and their brain develops. However, this will be a much simpler Operating System than one they may run on later on in life - or not.

For example, around the age of 4, your Operating System may be one of naughtiness. Most of the things you do will be triggered by your "Naughty" Operating System.

Some people call this your Personality. They can say, you have a naughty personality.

A this point, you are probably thinking, what is the difference between Personality and The Human Operating System. Are they not one and the same?

The concept of a Human Operating System (HOS) and Personality can be closely related, but they are not identical.

Here's a breakdown of their fundamental differences:

1. Nature vs. Mechanism

- **Personality**: This refers to the combination of characteristics or qualities that form an individual's distinctive character. It encompasses traits like openness, conscientiousness, extraversion, agreeableness, and neuroticism. Personality is a result of both genetic factors and environmental influences, shaping how a person thinks, feels, and behaves.

- **Human Operating System (HOS)**: This is a metaphorical framework suggesting that humans operate based on a set of (or one main) internal "programmes" or "scripts" that guide their actions and decisions. The HOS is more about the underlying processes and mechanisms that dictate behaviour, akin to software running on a computer.

2. Components vs. Structure

- **Personality**: Focuses on traits, which are stable characteristics that influence behaviour across various situations. It is often categorised using models like the Big Five (OCEAN: Openness, Conscientiousness, Extraversion, Agreeableness, Neuroticism).

- **HOS**: The HOS could be seen as the structure or architecture within which personality operates.

3. Stability vs. Adaptability

- **Personality**: Generally stable over time, though it can evolve with significant life experiences or deliberate effort.

- **HOS**: Implies a dynamic system that can be updated or reprogrammed. Just like software, parts of the HOS can be debugged, upgraded, or modified based on new inputs, learning, and self-awareness.

4. Focus on Outcomes vs. Processes

- **Personality**: Primarily descriptive, focusing on the what (e.g., what kind of person someone is).

- **HOS**: More prescriptive or explanatory, focusing on the how and why (e.g., how does this person make decisions, why do they behave in a certain way).

5. Observable vs. Internal Dynamics

- **Personality**: Largely observable through behaviour and self-reports, it provides a snapshot of consistent patterns.

- **HOS**: Emphasises the internal dynamics and processes, including unconscious mechanisms, cognitive biases, and emotional regulation systems that drive observable behaviour. Generally guided by one main commander.

6. Analogy to Technology

- **Personality**: Like the visible interface of a programme, what you see and interact with.

- **HOS**: Like the underlying code and algorithms that determine how the program runs and responds.

While personality provides a static view of an individual's traits and tendencies, the Human Operating System offers a dynamic and comprehensive framework that includes the processes and mechanisms driving those traits and behaviours. As you will see later on, the HOS is really just ONE main commander, for most people.

We will delve into this in more detail further along in the book. However the take from the above is that Personality is what you see with people. The Human Operating System is something you may not necessarily see when dealing with someone.

Internalising it, your personality is how you see yourself. Your Human Operating System is not clear to you unless you consciously search for it and identify it. How do you do that?

You do it with the help of this book.

Key Difference between Personality and The Human Operating System:

The Human Operating System is something you may not necessarily see when dealing with someone - whilst you may "see" their Personality. Internalising it, your personality is how you see yourself. Your Human Operating System is not clear to you unless you consciously search for it and identify it.

This book is going to give you the manual for identifying your own Secret Human Operating System and will enable you to utilise it to better yourself and achieve more of your goals. Those goals may be different from how your HOS is telling you to behave and act right now.

Furthermore, the beauty of knowing about The Secret Human Operating System is that you can use it to interact better with people and get more out of your relationships.

Can you change people using the HOS? Possibly by making them aware of their HOS or by acting on their HOS (even if not known to them - more later) but you need to be very conscious of the fact that it is near impossible to change one's Human Operating System.

WHAT? You ask!

Yes, it's true. If you were able to snap your fingers and change your HOS, then everyone would be who they want to be and achieve everything they ever wanted.

This is not to say it is not possible and hence why you are reading this book but just to give you this early caveat, you need to be aware that to change your HOS, you need to be extremely determined and have very specific reasons for why you want to change it and more importantly keep it changed. Human beings always revert back to their main Human Operating System no matter how many times they change it. This is why you have to be aware of the enormity of the task you are about to undertake.

If you want to run on a completely new Human Operating System, you need to have a very strong reason to want to make the change.

Some examples of the sort of "strong" reasons are below:

You are getting divorced and this is your last chance to change.

You are losing your house and livelihood and you need to change.

You are seriously ill because of the way you are/ think (smoking for example or mental illness) and you need to get well.

These are seriously strong reasons that can make people act and continue to act in a way to change their HOS.

Wanting more money, wanting to look cool or frivolous things with no specific aim are not enough to change one's HOS.

What is Personality?

Following on from the above differentiations, what is Personality exactly? It is important to not confuse the multi-faceted Personality with the often one dominator HOS.

You can change aspects of your personality and maybe even keep them changed. Changing your HOS is another matter.

Personality is a complex and multifaceted construct that comprises various elements. Here are the key components that collectively shape someone's personality:

1. Traits

- **Big Five Traits (OCEAN)**: Openness, Conscientiousness, Extraversion, Agreeableness, Neuroticism as mentioned already.
- **Other Traits**: Honesty-Humility, Emotionality, Social Boldness, Self-Discipline, etc.

2. Temperament

- **Basic Emotional Patterns**: Reactivity, self-regulation, intensity of emotional responses.
- **Early Developmental Influences**: Innate predispositions observable in infancy and early childhood.

3. Genetic Factors

- **Inherited Characteristics**: Traits passed down from parents, influencing temperament and predispositions.

4. Biological Factors

- **Brain Structure and Chemistry**: Neurotransmitter levels, brain activity patterns, hormonal influences.
- **Physiological Responses**: Heart rate variability, stress response systems.

5. Cognitive Patterns

- **Thought Processes**: Ways of thinking, problem-solving, decision-making styles.
- **Beliefs and Attitudes**: Core beliefs about the self, others, and the world.
- **Intelligence**: Cognitive abilities, including logical reasoning, creativity, and emotional intelligence.

6. Emotional Patterns

- **Emotional Stability**: Frequency and intensity of emotional experiences.
- **Emotion Regulation**: Ability to manage and respond to emotions in a healthy way.

7. Behavioural Patterns

- **Habits and Routines**: Consistent patterns of behaviour in various situations.
- **Response Tendencies**: Typical ways of reacting to challenges, opportunities, and stressors.

8. Motivational Factors

- **Drives and Needs**: Basic needs (e.g., Maslow's hierarchy), intrinsic and extrinsic motivations.
- **Goals and Aspirations**: Long-term objectives, ambitions, and personal projects.

9. Social Factors

- **Interpersonal Relationships**: Quality and nature of interactions with family, friends, colleagues.
- **Social Skills**: Communication abilities, empathy, assertiveness.
- **Cultural Influences**: Norms, values, and expectations from the cultural environment.

10. Environmental Influences

- **Upbringing and Family Environment**: Parenting style, family dynamics, early life experiences.
- **Education and Learning Experiences**: Formal education, life lessons, critical incidents.
- **Life Events**: Significant experiences, traumas, successes, and failures.

11. Experiential Factors

- **Life History**: Personal narrative, significant memories, and pivotal moments.
- **Adaptation and Coping Mechanisms**: Ways of dealing with stress, change, and adversity.

12. Self-Concept

- **Self-Image**: How individuals see themselves.
- **Self-Esteem**: Overall sense of self-worth.
- **Identity**: Sense of who one is, encompassing various roles and memberships (e.g., gender, nationality, profession).

13. Psychological Defence Mechanisms

- **Conscious and Unconscious Mechanisms**: Ways of protecting the self from psychological harm (e.g., denial, projection, rationalisation).

14. Values and Morals

- **Ethical Beliefs**: Standards of right and wrong, moral principles guiding behaviour.
- **Personal Values**: Core values that drive decisions and actions.

Personality is the interplay of traits, temperament, genetics, biology, cognition, emotion, behaviour, motivation, social and environmental factors, experiences, self-concept, defence mechanisms, and values. These elements interact dynamically, contributing to the unique and multifaceted nature of each individual's personality.

The Secret Human Operating System on the other hand can and should be broken down to in reality, ONE trait. The top level key driver in everything you do, including how your personality is shaped.

In reality, HOS sits on top of Personality and commands it. You may or may not be aware of it, but it is there, secretly hidden, driving your personality and the decisions you make and the way you are.

Once you identify your HOS, the world will become so much clearer to you and getting what you want in life will be much easier. Once you identify the HOS for others, you can deal with them much easier also and even get more of what you want out of them.

Remember, every person has a Human Operating System. Some clever people are aware of it. Most of us, are not.

The Human Operating System is the top level commander, controlling.. YOU!

It has been programmed into you possibly from birth, but more likely somewhere along your life. It can be as early as childhood or for many, later on in life. Maybe in your teens, twenties or sometimes later.

Who has programmed it into you?

YOU have! Maybe not consciously. Possibly through circumstances, repeat behaviour or nurture.
There is only ONE main HOS commanding you but there can be up to 3 other minor programmes running below or parallel to it and as with any human, many other smaller programmes below them. These are called Subsystems.

However, it is the main HOS that we are concerned with here; the Mothership. Your command centre.

How many Human Operating Systems are there?

That is the million dollar question. Remember, there will be overlap with other HOS if you look at the list. But out of the list, there will be ONE and only one HOS that truly dictates the majority of your decisions and explains the majority of your actions.

Remember your HOS can be one for your whole life or it can change from different periods. But for the most part, unless you are very aware of it, the changes are without you consciously making them. They are always out of your control and made without your full consent or active participation.

For example, you can be running on the HOS "Happy" for many years of your life. You may or may not be aware that your HOS is Happy.

Then, a life event or death of someone can change and reprogram your main HOS to "Grieving". This can go on for many years. You may even be aware that you are slightly sad or not your previous self.

However, it is only when you look at it from the HOS perspective, realising that your previous Human Operating System of Happy has now been replaced by Grieving, that you can actually start possibly doing something about it.

You have to recognise, respect and appreciate your Secret Human Operating System. Only then, you can do something about it to make your life better.

Without further ado, let's delve into the list of various Human Operating Systems that can be commanding you. These are not in any particular order:

Happy

Sad

Angry

Stressed

Calm

Relaxed

Anxious

- Excited
- Bored
- Curious
- Focused
- Distracted
- Tired
- Energetic
- Motivated
- Lazy
- Confused
- Clear-headed
- Fearful
- Brave
- Empathetic
- Visionary
- Apathetic
- Relaxed
- Jealous
- Content
- Grieving
- Elated

In Love

Heartbroken

Paranoid

Trusting

Cautious

Reckless

Confident

Insecure

Inspired

Creative

Genius

Forgetful

Inspirational

Attentive

Daydreaming

Innovative

Reflective

Impulsive

Patient

Irritable

Joyful

- Melancholic
- Indifferent
- Enthusiastic
- Nostalgic
- Adventurous
- Homesick
- Driven
- Lonely
- Sociable
- Introverted
- Extroverted
- Competitive
- Cooperative
- Pioneering
- Selfish
- Altruistic
- Imaginative
- Philanthropic
- Pessimistic
- Optimistic

Grateful

Resentful

Compassionate

Money-Obsessed

Forgiving

Vengeful

Overwhelmed

Underwhelmed

Menopausal

Pregnant

Maternal/Paternal

Protective

Neglectful

Sex-Obsessed

Asexual

Savvy

Romantic

Platonic

Ethical

Amoral

Spiritual

Determined

Skeptical

Guilty

Proud

Ashamed

Humble

Egoistic

Judgmental

Tolerant

Conventional

Courageous

Cowardly

Resilient

Gracious

Peaceful

Rude

Thankful

Charismatic

Ungrateful

Alert

- Family
- Drowsy
- Playful
- Serious
- Aggressive
- Passive
- Detached
- Engaged
- Cunning
- Morbid
- Evil
- Secretive
- Loyal
- Dramatic
- Negative
- Positive
- Religious
- Assertive
- Not Assertive

At this stage you may be thinking that you are many of these things. Either now, or at different times. You could also think these can be classed as your Personality.

Correct. They can be and yes you can have these are part of your personality. However, we are not here to look at them from that perspective. We are here to look at them as your HOS at this very minute; at this time in your life.

You need to have a good look at the list and as confusing as it may first be, you need to choose ONE of the above that you believe is the key dominator in your life's decisions and one that sits above your personality. There is no doubt that many, as much as 20 of these may all be contenders for this.

For example, you may be Angry and Negative. How do you choose?

You choose by seeing which one rules the majority of your life's decisions. The HOS that commands the Most decisions and areas in your life is the one which is truly at this moment at least, your true Secret Human Operating System - soon to be not so secret!

If you are finding it difficult to choose, then you can try the following experiment.

How to find your Secret Human Operating System

Write down on a piece of paper several words from the above list that are possibly your main HOS but that you can't decide on. Narrow down, say 10 of the above words.

Now, write down 10 recent decisions you have made or recent interactions you have had. They can be anything from an argument, to the decision to buy something or choosing to go or not to go to an event.

For example, "The time I went to a car show but decided to leave early."

Then, underneath each interaction/decision, write down which of the possible HOS could have been the driving factor in the main decisions. Try and put the most relevant one(s) at the top.

For example, you had an argument with a builder outside your house. It could have been because your HOS is Angry or Sad. How do you choose? Write both down.

Then for example, you were upset with your partner. Again, maybe you were Angry too but in reality, it was because you were Menopausal. So write down Menopausal, not Angry.

If you do this for many of the recent decisions and interactions you have had, you will find a pattern and you will end up with ONE key driver. One main word will eventually keep popping up. If you can't find it, keep writing experiences and populating the relevant words underneath.
Once you have found that one word that keeps recurring, this is your current Human Operating System.

It may have been your HOS all your life or for the last few months of years. Only you will know that by analysing it. Remember, the HOS is not your Personality. You may be "nice" or "evil" or something else.

Your HOS is what drives most of your decisions. So, let's say your HOS is Rude. Then pretty much most of your life's decisions and interactions will be ruled by that.

Do bear in mind that some Human Operating System main driver's are not as powerful as others. Just like a computer, the main command programme may not be as powerful for some as others.

Following the above example, Rude is not as powerful as Genius.

Rude may be commanding many aspects of your life as a HOS, but several other smaller HOS subsystems sitting underneath may be taking over for certain areas of your life for you to make decisions and function.

You can be Rude many times and make many decisions based on your HOS being that of Rude. However, these interactions and decisions will be a lot less frequent than if your Human Operating System was Genius.

With Genius, many of your life's events and actions will be dictated by this powerful Human Operating System.

You may ask, what is the point of learning about the Human Operating System if you find out that your one is not worthy of change or attention for whatever reason?

The answer is, ALL Human Operating Systems are worthy of recognition and attention.

Once you recognise them and act on this recognition, you can quite literally change your life.

If you realise your HOS is Rude, you will suddenly realise why you do the things you do. Why you make the decisions you make. Why you feel the way you do before, during and after life's events. Why you come across the way you do. Why people treat you in a certain way and why you treat them in a particular way. Why you do or probably more often than not, don't get what you want! Why your life has ended up the way it has.

If someone blocks your driveway and your HOS is Rude, you will be commanded to act in a Rude, aggressive, disrespectful way which may end up not serving you well.

If your HOS is Genius and someone blocks your driveway, you may interact with them and find out the motivation for their act and find a Genius way of getting what you want out of them i.e. removal of their vehicle.

The above is just one example. Once you become aware of your HOS, and you learn to constantly remind yourself of the fact that it is driving you, you can question your decisions and see if they are guided correctly in alignment with what you REALLY want out of life.

Recognising your HOS is only the beginning. The next part for most people is whether this HOS is serving them well in their life.

Chances are, if your HOS is Genius, it is probably serving you well in life for the most part. But everyone is different. One person running on HOS Genius, may be super happy and content especially if they recognise they are running on Genius.

Another person running on Genius may be horrified and may want to truly change their HOS to something else, like "Content", for example.

Once you have recognised your Secret Human Operating System, you need to decide whether it is serving you or standing in your way.

For most people, it can be changed totally or the subsystems sitting under the main HOS can be replaced.

If a person is 100% happy with their HOS (which is rare for all their life) then, that is fine. They can keep it as it is and tweak the subsystems.

How do you find out what are the main 2 or 3 subsystems sitting under your HOS?

By following the exact method described above but for a subsystem.

So you would write down some recent actions and decisions and ignoring the main big, sitting there in your face HOS, you look for other more frequently appearing words.

If your main HOS is Angry, maybe you start seeing Unhappy, Impulsive or other words appearing more frequently in the exercise to determine your HOS or Subsystem.

The top most appearing words, are your subsystems. Most people run on a main HOS and 2-3 subsystems for most of their life decisions and interactions. However, some people are more complex and they may run on several subsystems.

The trick here is not to get too bogged down with tens of subsystems! You need to be focused and ideally identify your main Secret Human Operating System.

If this SHOS is not serving you and you are aware of this, then you need to change it (more later). If your SHOS is serving you for the most part, then you need to start looking at changing the subsystems if they can be replaced with more productive ones.

Below is a list of some famous people and we have second-guessed their Secret Operating System.

Elon Musk - Visionary
Oprah Winfrey - Inspirational
Albert Einstein - Genius
Steve Jobs - Innovative
Mother Teresa - Compassionate
Muhammad Ali - Courageous
Warren Buffett - Savvy
Nelson Mandela - Resilient
Mark Zuckerberg - Ambitious
Marie Curie - Pioneering
Leonardo da Vinci - Creative
Malala Yousafzai - Brave
Barack Obama - Charismatic
J.K. Rowling - Imaginative
Amelia Earhart - Adventurous
Bill Gates - Philanthropic
Serena Williams - Determined
Galileo Galilei - Curious
Mahatma Gandhi - Peaceful
Jeff Bezos - Driven

Notice the HOS can change over time. Bill Gates could have been running on Visionary or Genius for many years before his HOS was switched to Philanthropic.

Could you run on any of the above? Have a think! What would it change in your life if you did?

Is your Secret Human Operating System negatively or positively affecting YOU or others?

This is an extremely difficult and complex question if you were to really sit down and think about it.

For example, your SHOS could be Lazy. It can be serving you well. You like being lazy, you like not doing much, you are a slob, you don't work much, you lazy about and you are happy!

However your HOS (or SHOH if you are not aware yet) can be dramatically affecting your relationship with your partner. This can just be affecting "them" solely or leading all the way to affecting you in the form of arguments and separation.

Complex? Yes because a separation can be good for your HOS in that you can go back to being Lazy all by yourself, or it can offset you and dramatically affect other aspects of your life, such as happiness or finances.

Being aware of your SHOS is the first step. Choosing to do something about changing it or its subsystems is the next stage.

We ask whether your SHOH is affecting YOU positively or negatively, inwards or outwards? i.e. with your relationship with the world.

Ultimately, you need to be the judge of that. Once you recognise your SHOS, you can decide how it is driving your life and in what direction (if at all) or for better or worse.

Not everyone wants to change. Not everyone cares. However, the fact that you are reading this book is a very good indicator that you do want to make changes to your life to become a better person and achieve more of the goals you have been wanting to achieve.

It really doesn't matter whether your HOS is affecting you or others. Everyone is different. The fact that you think you may need to change it or its subsystems means it is not 100% benefiting you.

2.
HOW CAN YOU CHANGE YOUR HUMAN OPERATING SYSTEM?

The greatest question before the "how" is "why"? Depending on how your Human Operating System is serving you at this stage in your life, you are probably inclined to ask, should you in fact want to change your HOS? Why should you?

Once the "why" question is answered, you can then look at the how.

Is your current Human Operating System serving you well in life?

It very much depends on what sort of person you are, which guess what? Goes back to what is your Human Operating System! Confusing, isn't it!

For example, if your HOS is "Tolerant", then you may well want to stick to everything in life, because you are Tolerant. It will only be because of something like this book or a major life event (fed up with being pushed around by your boss) that you may want to change it. By the way, a major life event may not be enough, so we are back to this book for help!

You would traditionally want to change your HOS because you are not achieving the things you want in life. You are not reaching your goals. You are not happy. You are not waking up with zest for life or going to sleep content.

It may not even be as dramatic. Or it could be even more dramatic. Everyone is different.

You change your Human Operating System by first Identifying it.

If you have been reading the previous chapter correctly and applying the principles, by now you should know what your primary dominant HOS is. You should also know what your 2-3 subsystems are.

Let's give you an example of a real life person, Alan.

Alan was in his 50s. He had been very successful in life and was content but more and more, he realised he was in fact empty inside. He did not wake up every day jumping for joy and was mostly unhappy.

Of course, success is defined by many things - according to people's personalities, expectations, surroundings and also HOS.

Success can also mean different things to the same person at different times. This is why it is important to first:

Have a goal

Then:

Find out your HOS

Then:
Compare your actual achievements with your goal.

You can then get more involved with how your HOS is affecting your level of success.

Coming back to Alan, upon a relatively simple test, this is what his results came back as:

Primary HOS was Egoistic. He was at the very basic part of his operating system egotistical and self centred. The majority of his life's decisions were made according to his ego. "Egoistic" is a big juicy HOS by the way; a real dominator! One of the biggest and most difficult to change.

Alan also had some subsystems which were:

Money-Obsessed
Nostalgic
Dramatic

These were 3 big subsystems for him; quite major players in his life.

Obviously, like most humans, he had many other characteristics which one could put under "Personality". But we won't bother with them here.

It is important for the purposes of this book to stick to what is your Human Operating System. NOT parts of your personality.

Upon fully realising that his main SHOS was Egoistic, Alan decided to go about trying to change it.

This was a near impossible task at first. How do you change your main Motherboard?! The thing that drives you and makes you operate the way you are and has been for decades? It is difficult.

You may find reasons to change, you may even succeed for a while but inevitably, you will reset back to the main current HOS. That is, if you are most people, if you are not aware of your HOS and if you haven't read this chapter!

Alan, like most people who succeed in changing their Human Operating System had to find a strong enough reason to actually upgrade or change his HOS.

He found this reason in the form of a new wife and family. This gave him purpose and reason to put aside his Egoistic HOS and replace it with "Family".

When you restart or shut down a computer, the operating system (OS) temporarily halts its processes and then reboots them when it starts up again. It's like you sleeping and waking up in the morning.

This process is akin to turning off a light switch and then turning it back on— it doesn't change the underlying components or the way the OS functions fundamentally. The hardware remains the same, and the core software configurations are reset to the state they were in before the restart. Therefore, any issues or behaviours that were present before the restart typically remain unchanged unless they were caused by temporary glitches or memory issues that are cleared by the restart.

On the other hand, changing the operating system can fundamentally transform the computer's behaviour and functionality. The OS is the software layer that manages the hardware and provides the platform for applications to run. Each operating system has its own set of drivers, services, and application interfaces, which determine how hardware is utilised and how software interacts with the system.

When you switch from one OS to another, you're often changing the entire environment in which the computer operates. For instance, moving from Windows to Linux, or from macOS to Windows, involves replacing not just the user interface but also the underlying system architecture, file management, security protocols, and available software ecosystems. This can lead to significant changes in performance, compatibility, and usability.

The computer effectively becomes a different machine in terms of how it processes information, interacts with users, and supports various applications and peripherals.

You wouldn't just change a computer's Operating System would you? And guess what? It is not done very often. Just like humans.

You would only do it if there was a very significant reason to do so.

Let there be no mistake, it takes a very unique individual to consciously change their HOS. For most of us, to change our HOS and keep it changed is near impossible.

It is important to understand this and the task that lays ahead. The word consciously is used because sometimes people's HOS changes without much effort on their part.

Take the case of Suri. She was a 23 year old graduate who had been extremely promiscuous from a young age. Her HOS was Sex-Obsessed. Everything she did was because she was running on the HOS of Sex-Obsessed.

She would miss lessons to have sex. She would go out to have sex. She lived because her primary HOS was commanding her to do exactly what she was doing. Can you see why this is very different from "Personality"? She had a nice personality. But even though "Nice" can be an HOS, in this instance, Sex-Obsessed was her main life's HOS.

How did she overcome such a powerful HOS? Sadly in her case and without her control, she had a stroke. A stroke in her early twenties totally and completely changed her HOS.

Last we heard, she was a mother with 2 kids and a career as an art critic.

Sometimes a Human Operating System can also change with time, but this is probably not the answer you are looking for.

In your teens and early life you can be Aggressive and this can be your main HOS, dictating, driving and perhaps ruining many aspects of your life and happiness.

As you age, your HOS can totally change and become Passive or something else, even Sex-Obsessed like the previous example. This is not an example of you consciously changing your path and your life. It is just how it goes for some or many people eventually.

When you find the strongest WHY, you can then change your Human Operating System.

The million dollar question being how do you find the strongest "why"? And most importantly, how do you get motivated in the first place to go looking for that why?

This is where most people fail and why most people are mediocre in life and they never get to their full potential. It all comes down to your goals.

The exercise you need to do for this chapter is very important. You need to grab some paper and a pen and write down your main top goal in life. It doesn't matter if it is unrealistic. Write it down. Obviously it can't be something silly like "I want to be a Martian". It has to be realistic, even if very far fetched.

Everyone has different goals in life. Your goal has to be specific to you. This is VERY important because it is YOUR Human Operating System that we will be trying to change to achieve YOUR goals.

However, if you have trouble with your imagination or you are not sure, here are 100 goals that have been set by others, to give you an idea:

Earn £10 million through investments and entrepreneurship.

Start a successful tech company.

Run a marathon in under 3 hours.

Write and publish a bestselling novel.

Build and live in a self-sustainable eco-friendly house.

Climb Mount Everest.

Become fluent in five languages.

Create a philanthropic foundation to help disadvantaged communities.

Win an Olympic medal.

Travel to every country in the world.

Create a viral YouTube channel with millions of subscribers.

Become a renowned motivational speaker.

Win a Nobel Prize in a chosen field.

Establish a successful art gallery.

Develop a cure for a major disease.

Design a revolutionary new technology or product.

Become a renowned chef and open a Michelin-starred restaurant.

Create a successful fashion line.

Become a top influencer on social media.

Earn a PhD in a challenging field.

Compose a symphony performed by a major orchestra.

Become a professional athlete in a chosen sport.

Build a successful online education platform.

Win a major international film festival award.

Start a successful non-profit organisation.

Become a leading expert in a specialised scientific field.

Write and direct a successful feature film.

Create a globally recognised brand.

Develop an influential podcast with millions of listeners.

Win a Pulitzer Prize for journalism.

Become a professional musician with a hit album.

Establish a chain of successful businesses.

Design and patent an innovative product.

Become a respected professor at a top university.

Develop a popular video game.

Start a successful travel blog.

Become an acclaimed actor or actress.

Build a state-of-the-art research facility.

Write a series of successful children's books.

Create a widely-used mobile app.

Become a recognised leader in environmental conservation.

Establish a major cultural festival.

Design a groundbreaking architectural structure.

Win a major literary award.

Become a successful real estate developer.

Launch a space-related venture.

Become a world champion in a chosen sport.

Create a groundbreaking educational curriculum.

Invent a new form of sustainable energy.

Produce a successful television series.

Become an influential political leader.

Create a major art installation.

Win a Grammy Award.

Become a leading expert in artificial intelligence.

Develop a major software platform.

Write a highly influential academic paper.

Create a world-renowned sculpture.

Become a famous landscape photographer.

Create an influential economic theory.

Develop a successful fitness brand.

Become a top-tier professional dancer.

Build a revolutionary transportation system.

Create a highly successful franchise.

Become a leading figure in global health initiatives.

Develop a successful wildlife conservation program.

Create a top-selling board game.

Become an acclaimed painter with exhibitions worldwide.

Design a successful fashion accessory.

Create a popular healthy food brand.

Develop a cutting-edge medical device.

Start a successful wine or spirits brand.

Become a leading expert in renewable energy.

Create a revolutionary educational tool.

Develop a highly popular social media platform.

Write an influential political theory book.

Create a globally successful health and wellness retreat.

Develop a successful financial technology company.

Become a renowned urban planner.

Create a major entertainment park.

Develop a leading e-commerce platform.

Write a critically acclaimed play.

Become a famous home designer.

Develop a successful agribusiness.

Create a popular luxury brand.

Become a world-renowned architect.

Develop a successful biotech company.

Create a groundbreaking robotics company.

Write a successful biography of a famous person.

Develop a major cultural initiative.

Become a top-tier chef with a cooking show.

Create a successful line of educational toys.

Develop a widely used mental health app.

Become an acclaimed wildlife filmmaker.

Create a successful line of eco-friendly products.

Develop a major sustainable agriculture project.

Become a leading figure in human rights advocacy.

Create a major historical documentary.

Develop a widely adopted clean water solution.

Write a series of successful self-help books.

Create a major global peace initiative.

Goals can be specific or broad but the more specific, the more chance of you being able to change your Human Operating System to align it with your goal(s).

The more emotion you associate with your goal, the more chances of success.

For example, rather than having a goal of "I want to marry". It is better to have a goal of "I want to marry Gina, my next door neighbour by this time next year."

Find out and give reasons to yourself as to WHY, you want this top-level goal. It can be several goals but the top level one is the most important.

Take Suraj. He was poor all his life. In his early thirties, he decided that enough was enough and he could literally not stand another minute of being poor.

He wanted money, security and all the things he kept dreaming about all his life. This was not his shut down and restart moment. This was not his reboot moment. This was a moment when he would be changing his entire Human Operating System forever.

Are your ready to have a strong enough goal and an even stronger WHY to be able to permanently change your Human Operating System?

The power of emotions

Achieving goals is a complex process influenced by various factors, and one of the most critical elements is emotional attachment. Emotions can serve as powerful motivators, driving us towards our objectives with greater intensity and determination. Below, we will explore how attaching emotions to your goals can increase the likelihood of success, the types of emotions that are most effective, and strategies to enhance the emotional connection to your goals.

Understanding Emotional Attachment

Emotional attachment to a goal means feeling a strong, often visceral connection to the outcome you desire. This connection can make the goal feel more meaningful and urgent, which in turn can fuel your motivation and persistence. Emotions can transform a mere objective into a compelling mission, increasing your commitment to seeing it through.

Types of Emotions That Drive Success

Not all emotions are created equal when it comes to achieving goals. Positive emotions generally provide the most effective motivational fuel. Here are some key emotions to consider:

- **Passion:** A deep-seated enthusiasm for your goal can keep you engaged and energised, even during challenging times.
- **Hope:** Believing in the possibility of achieving your goal can sustain your motivation and help you overcome setbacks.
- **Pride:** Anticipating the pride you'll feel upon achieving your goal can drive you to work harder and persevere.
- **Joy:** Visualising the happiness and satisfaction you'll experience can make the process more enjoyable and keep you focused.
- **Gratitude:** Feeling grateful for the opportunity to pursue your goal can enhance your overall well-being and motivation.

How to Attach Emotions to Your Goals

1. **Visualise Success:** Spend time each day visualising the successful achievement of your goal. Picture the details vividly and focus on the emotions you'll experience. This mental rehearsal can make the goal feel more real and emotionally charged.

2. **Connect with Your Why:** Understand the deeper reasons behind your goal. Ask yourself why it's important to you and what achieving it will mean for

your life. The stronger your personal reasons, the more emotional weight your goal will carry.

3. **Use Affirmations:** Create positive affirmations related to your goal. Repeat them daily to reinforce your emotional connection and build a positive mindset.

4. **Share Your Goal:** Talk about your goal with supportive friends, family, or mentors. Sharing your aspirations can enhance your commitment and the emotional investment you have in achieving them.

5. **Celebrate Milestones:** Recognise and celebrate small victories along the way. Each milestone reached should be a source of joy and pride, reinforcing your emotional attachment and keeping your motivation high.

Enhancing the Emotional Connection

To make your emotional attachment even more powerful, consider these advanced strategies:

- **Create a Vision Board:** A visual representation of your goal can serve as a constant reminder of what you're working towards. Fill it with images and words that evoke strong positive emotions.
- **Incorporate Sensory Experiences:** Engage your senses in your goal-setting process. Play music that inspires you, use scents that relax and motivate you, and engage in physical activities that boost your mood.
- **Practice Mindfulness:** Stay present and connected to your emotions throughout your goal journey. Mindfulness can help you stay aware of your motivations and keep your emotions aligned with your objectives.

- **Write a Goal Narrative:** Compose a detailed narrative describing your journey to achieving your goal. Include the challenges you'll face, how you'll overcome them, and the emotions you'll experience. Reading this narrative regularly can reinforce your emotional commitment.

Finding the WHY is only part of the journey.

So far,

1. We have found out what our HOS is
2. We have set a GOAL and decided on achieving it
3. We have found the strongest WHY for the goal and attached emotions to it

Next, you need to decide what Human Operating System is going to serve you better than all the rest of them in achieving your goal.

How to choose your next Human Operating System to change your life, happiness and destiny?

This is indeed a very important decision. So many to choose from! Where do you even start?

It is actually not as complex as you may think. In a way, choosing your WHY is more difficult than choosing your goal and your next HOS.

You need to think of your next Human Operating System as not just the driver to most of your life's decisions, but as the main driver to your goal.

Going back to Suraj's example, his whole life had been under the HOS of "Grateful". Sure, he was happy, he was content, he was... Grateful! But this is not what he REALLY wanted and at that stage in his life in his thirties, he decided that the HOS that would really serve him is in fact "Money-Obsessed". This is the HOS of a great many successful people by the way. It is a powerful one when installed properly and run at full power.

When your HOS is Money-Obsessed it rules and drives every life decision. It may not be the most pretty HOS or the most kind, but boy is it a strong one! It hammers through life's problems and obstacles because ultimately, you are money-obsessed and everything you do will be to serve your HOS of money obsession.

Your choice for your next HOS must drive at least 80% of your decisions without hesitation, without uncertainty and without problems in your conscience.

If your HOS has been Passive, you may now choose Active. However, you have to realise that this HOS must dominate and dictate everything.

If you have been a "lurker" on social media because of your Passive HOS, now you will be an active participant and contributor if you were to change your HOS to Active.

If you used to go to a bar and just sit and wait to be served, now with an Active HOS you will go to the front, get a drink, talk to whoever you want and make things happen.

If you have been the type to not get into a packed train because of your Passive HOS, now you will go and squeeze in no matter how packed the carriage is.

A newly chosen HOS is like a new personality but much more powerful, much more of a driver and much more effective.

Look at the list of the various Human Operating Systems in chapter one and choose the one that will BEST serve your new goals.

If you are finding it very hard to choose just one, then do the following exercise:

How to choose a new Human Operating System for yourself

Imagine yourself in several scenarios which involve your new goal. You can write them down on a piece of paper. For example, following from the Gina neighbour example of the above:

1. I am in my garden and I see Gina in hers, next door.
2. I run into Gina at the local coffee shop.
3. I want to attract the attention of Gina somehow.

Then write a narrowed down top 10 list of the best HOS you can think of for each scenario and to get an effective outcome.

The more scenarios you write down based on your main goal, the better. You will soon find that one particular HOS (in this case Secret Operation System before it is discovered, by you!) will appear more often and THIS will be your main new lead HOS.

Depending on the sort of person, goal and WHY, you may find 2-3 other subsystem HOSs also appearing in the lists numerous times. These will be your subsystems for your new goal.

However, never forget that the most important aspect of achieving your goals, NOW, more than ever is the new chosen Human Operating System that will dominate everything you do from now on in life. It needs to be chosen carefully and needs to remain in power.

3.
HOW TO HAVE BETTER INTERACTIONS WITH OTHERS

Your Secret Human Operating System is not so secret when you figure out exactly what yours is at the present time and what you are running on.

Once you are fully aware of it, you may even look back and realise what Human Operating System you were running on at different times of your life.

Finding our what HOS you are running on is key to making personal changes and realising your goals.

As you would expect, others are also running on their own HOS. Theirs is definitely a secret to you and probably to them!

Whilst with your new knowledge, you may think that you can second-guess what HOS others are running on, you have to be careful.

What may seem like an obvious HOS for someone, may not be so correct in actual terms. For example, you may see someone and think their HOS is Aggressive or Kind, but in actual fact, it can be "Overwhelmed". This could be triggering and running most of their processes and life decisions, including ones to do with you. Kind can just be their personality or facade!

How do you have better interactions with others? The obvious answer is to find out what HOS they are running on - NOT their personality. Once you figure the HOS out, things become easier in developing better relations with them.

"They" can be anyone. Your partner, your family, your friends, a colleague or even an adversary. It can even be someone you run into just once.

On a simpler level without thinking of the Human Operating System, it is said that:

If you can figure out someone's motivation, you can figure out how they will act.

Motivation is similar to the Human Operating System in the case of other people. It is probably easier to figure out their motivation than their HOS. Everyone has secrets and things you (and even they) may not be aware of.

You may be thinking that once you figure out someone's HOS, then you can just deal with them more efficiently and effectively. Right?

Sort of! It's a little bit more complicated than that and as you may expect, it will require a bit more effort on your part! Otherwise everyone would be amazing at interpersonal relationships and getting what they want.

They key to having better interpersonal relationships and pretty much getting your way, is to not only second-guess people's HOS as accurately as you can, but in 80% of cases, to <u>ADAPT it as your own when dealing with them</u>.

That sounds a little bit crazy, right? Run their Operating System over yours?

In Neuro-Linguistic Programming (NLP - more later) they may call this process just described as Mirroring. Mirroring in itself is an extremely powerful tool and very effective.

Mirroring involves mimicking the behaviour, body language, speech patterns, and attitudes of another person. The primary goal of mirroring is to build rapport, create a sense of connection, and facilitate better communication. By subtly reflecting the actions and speech of another person, one can foster trust and mutual understanding, which can be particularly beneficial in various professional and personal interactions.

How is Mirroring Done?

Mirroring can be applied in several ways, focusing on different aspects of communication:

1. **Body Language:**

- **Posture**: Adopt a similar posture to the person you are interacting with. If they are sitting with their legs crossed, you might do the same.
- **Gestures**: Use similar hand gestures or movements. If they frequently use their hands while speaking, try to do so as well.
- **Facial Expressions**: Reflect their facial expressions to show empathy and understanding. If they smile, smile back.

2. **Speech Patterns:**

    - **Tone and Pitch**: Match the tone and pitch of their voice. If they speak softly, lower your voice accordingly.
    - **Pacing and Rhythm**: Adjust the speed and rhythm of your speech to align with theirs. If they speak slowly, slow down your speech.
    - **Language and Vocabulary**: Use similar words and phrases. If they use specific jargon or terminology, incorporate those into your conversation.

3. **Attitudes and Emotions:**

    - **Emotional State**: Reflect their emotional state. If they are enthusiastic, show enthusiasm in your responses.
    - **Attitude**: Mirror their attitudes and opinions subtly. If they express optimism, align your conversation to reflect a positive outlook.

Benefits of Mirroring

1. **Building Rapport:**

    - Mirroring creates a sense of familiarity and comfort, helping to establish a strong connection between individuals.
    - It fosters trust and openness, making others feel understood and valued.

2. **Improved Communication:**

    - Enhances the flow of conversation by reducing barriers and misunderstandings.
    - Encourages more effective and empathetic listening.

3. **Influence and Persuasion:**

    - By creating a sense of alignment, mirroring can make it easier to influence and persuade others.
    - People are more likely to be receptive to suggestions from someone they feel connected to.

4. **Conflict Resolution:**

    - Helps in de-escalating conflicts by creating a cooperative and empathetic environment.
    - Facilitates better negotiation and problem-solving by ensuring all parties feel heard and respected.

Effects of Mirroring

1. **Positive Effects**:
    - **Enhanced Relationships**: Strengthens personal and professional relationships by fostering mutual respect and understanding.
    - **Increased Cooperation**: Promotes teamwork and collaboration in group settings.
    - **Greater Empathy**: Enhances emotional intelligence and the ability to empathise with others.

2. **Potential Negative Effects**:
    - **Over-Mirroring**: If done too obviously, mirroring can appear insincere or manipulative, leading to distrust.
    - **Misuse**: When used with ill intentions, mirroring can be manipulative and may harm relationships.

Mirroring in NLP is a subtle yet effective technique for enhancing communication and building rapport. By reflecting the behaviour, speech, and attitudes of others, individuals can create a sense of connection and trust that facilitates better interactions. When used appropriately, mirroring can lead to numerous benefits, including improved relationships, increased influence, and more effective conflict resolution.

With Mirroring, you are being very effective but you are not going deep into finding out the person's HOS. You are simply getting what you want, coaxing, manipulating and nudging to achieve a better outcome for yourself.

With The Human Operating System, you are getting at the most basic, command centre of the person.

However, you are not trying to do some complex analysis. You are going to run THIER operating system and let it override yours when you are interacting with them; you will do this only for the time you are interacting with them either in person or by other means (text, email, call etc).

Reading this at first, may sound puzzling, so let's break it down and then give you some examples.

How do you find out the other person's Secret Human Operating System?

You look for clues. That's the best you can do. They are not going to tell you their HOS and chances are, they won't even know what you are talking about and even if they did, they probably wouldn't know their HOS.

You have to come a level (or several levels) down from the HOS and look for things in their Personality, Motivation and possibly subsystems that may be overtly clear to you.

For this, you can use NLP. We have mentioned NLP already, but many of you may not know what NLP is, so let's delve deeper into this and then we will look at how NLP can be used to find out people's motivations and drivers and ultimately, take a best guess at their HOS.

What is Neuro-Linguistic Programming (NLP)?

Neuro-Linguistic Programming (NLP) is a psychological approach that explores the connections between neurological processes ("neuro"), language ("linguistic"), and behavioural patterns learned through experience ("programming"). It is based on the premise that these three components can be modified to achieve specific goals in life, improve communication, and foster personal development.

Origins and Inventors

NLP was developed in the 1970s by Richard Bandler and John Grinder at the University of California, Santa Cruz. Bandler was a student of psychology and computer science, while Grinder was an associate professor of linguistics. They aimed to create a methodology that could model the skills of exceptional people, enabling others to acquire those skills.

Key Concepts and Techniques

1. **Modelling**: Studying the behaviour and thought patterns of successful individuals to replicate their success.
2. **Rapport**: Building a connection and trust with others through techniques like mirroring and matching.
3. **Anchoring**: Associating a specific stimulus with a particular emotional state or behaviour.
4. **Reframing**: Changing the way a situation or behaviour is perceived to alter its meaning and effect.
5. **Submodalities**: Examining the finer details of sensory experiences to change perceptions and responses.
6. **Meta-Programs**: Understanding the unconscious filters people use to process information.

Successful Applications of NLP

NLP has been used successfully in various fields including therapy, business, sports, and personal development. Here are some notable applications:

1. **Therapy**: NLP techniques have been used to help individuals overcome phobias, anxiety, depression, and other psychological issues.
2. **Business**: NLP is utilised for improving communication, leadership skills, sales techniques, and team building.
3. **Sports**: Athletes use NLP to enhance performance, focus, and mental resilience.
4. **Education**: Teachers and trainers apply NLP to improve teaching methods and facilitate better learning experiences.
5. **Personal Development**: Individuals use NLP for goal setting, self-motivation, and personal growth.

Examples of NLP in Use

1. **Therapeutic Context**: A therapist might use NLP techniques to help a client overcome a fear of public speaking by anchoring a feeling of confidence to a specific gesture.
2. **Business Setting**: A sales professional might use mirroring and matching to build rapport with potential clients, making them feel more comfortable and increasing the likelihood of a sale.
3. **Sports Coaching**: A coach might use visualisation techniques from NLP to help an athlete mentally rehearse successful performance, enhancing their actual performance during competition.

Famous People Who Have Used NLP

1. **Tony Robbins**: The renowned motivational speaker and life coach has integrated NLP into his personal development seminars and coaching practices.

Robbins learned NLP directly from Richard Bandler and has popularised its techniques.
2. **Bill Clinton**: Former U.S. President Bill Clinton is said to have used NLP techniques for effective communication and public speaking.
3. **Oprah Winfrey**: The media mogul has used NLP principles in her personal development and self-help programs.
4. **Andre Agassi**: The tennis champion has reportedly used NLP techniques to improve his mental game and performance on the court.

Neuro-Linguistic Programming is a versatile and influential approach that has been applied successfully in various fields. By understanding and manipulating the connections between neurological processes, language, and behaviour, individuals can achieve greater personal and professional success. The techniques of NLP, from modelling to anchoring, offer powerful tools for improving communication, overcoming psychological barriers, and fostering personal growth.

You can use NLP to decipher people's Human Operating System.

How can NLP be used to find out people's Motivations and take a best guess at their HOS?

Understanding People's Motivation and Desires

1. **Active Listening and Observation**:
    - Pay close attention to their language, tone, and body language.

- Notice the words they use frequently, as these can indicate their values and beliefs.

2. **Asking the Right Questions**:
   - Use open-ended questions to encourage them to share more about themselves.
   - Questions like "What is important to you about...?" or "What do you hope to achieve with...?" can reveal their underlying motivations.

3. **Meta-Programs**:
   - Identify their meta-programs, which are the unconscious filters through which people process information.
   - Common meta-programs include:
     - **Toward vs. Away From**: Are they motivated by goals and aspirations (toward) or by avoiding problems and pain (away from)?
     - **Options vs. Procedures**: Do they prefer having choices and flexibility (options) or following a set process (procedures)?
     - **Internal vs. External Frame of Reference**: Do they rely on their own judgment (internal) or seek validation from others (external)?

Techniques to Uncover Motivations

1. **Elicitation of Values**:
   - Values are core motivators. To elicit values, ask questions such as:
     - "What is important to you in your career/relationship/life?"
     - "What do you value most about...?"

- Listen for key values that drive their behaviour.

2. **Well-Formed Outcomes**:

    - Help them articulate their goals in a specific, positive, and achievable manner.
    - Use the SMART criteria (Specific, Measurable, Achievable, Relevant, Time-bound) to refine their goals.
    - Questions to ask include:
        - "What exactly do you want to achieve?"
        - "How will you know when you have achieved it?"

3. **Perceptual Positions**:

    - Use perceptual positions to understand their perspective and those of others involved.
    - First Position: Their own perspective.
    - Second Position: The perspective of the other person.
    - Third Position: An objective observer's viewpoint.
    - This technique helps uncover hidden motivations and improve empathy.

Improving Interaction Based on Motivations

1. **Matching and Mirroring**:

    - Reflect their body language, speech patterns, and attitudes to build rapport.
    - This creates a sense of connection and makes them feel understood.

2. **Language Patterns:**
    - Use the same language and terminology they use to create a deeper connection.
    - For example, if they often talk about "achieving success," incorporate similar phrases in your conversation.

3. **Reframing:**
    - Reframe their concerns or objections in a positive light.
    - For instance, if they are worried about failure, reframe it as an opportunity to learn and grow.

4. **Anchoring:**
    - Use anchoring to create positive emotional states.
    - Anchor positive feelings to specific words, gestures, or objects that can be used to trigger those states in the future.

5. **Chunking:**
    - Use chunking up or down to match their level of detail.
    - Chunking up: Discuss broader concepts and generalities if they prefer big-picture thinking.
    - Chunking down: Focus on specifics and details if they prefer granular information.

Practical Steps to Implement NLP Techniques

1. **Build Rapport:**
    - Establish a connection by matching and mirroring their behaviour and language.

- Ensure your interactions are genuine and respectful.

2. **Identify Motivational Drivers**:
    - Use elicitation techniques to uncover their core values and goals.
    - Listen for cues in their language and observe their behaviour.

3. **Align Your Communication**:
    - Tailor your communication style to match their preferences and motivations.
    - Use appropriate language patterns, chunking, and reframing techniques.

4. **Provide Support and Encouragement**:
    - Reinforce their positive states and provide encouragement towards their goals.
    - Use anchoring to create lasting positive associations.

By employing these NLP techniques, you can gain a deeper understanding of what drives individuals, what they truly want, and how you can interact with them more effectively.

You can find many books on NLP and it is an incredibly powerful tool for everything in life.

Now, we get to something that you will not find in most NLP or other books. That is what we touched on earlier, which is replacing your own HOS with someone's else's when dealing with them. This will work in 80% of cases (more on the 20% shortly).

When we speak of dealing with others, we are referring to trying to have the most effective communication you can have and getting what you want out of that relationship either in person or remotely.

Here's an example:

Samantha, the unhappy wife.

Derek had tried everything to make it work with his wife Samantha but as much as they had happy times, it would always end up with them being close to getting divorced.

Derek just couldn't figure out where he was going wrong. Neither of them were perfect in many ways and possibly not perfect for each other but as a last try, Derek decided to try The Human Operating System and took the drastic measure of replacing his own HOS, which was "Determined" with Samantha's. Sounds like a scene from Dracula, right!

Samantha's HOS was "Happiness". Derek made life simpler for himself by calling her HOS simply, Samantha. Whenever he was dealing with his wife, he replaced his own HOS with that of Samantha.

Instead of shouting, he would think what would serve Samantha's HOS "Happiness". Instead of reacting, going out with his mates, lazying about and being "himself", he would consciously and with much effort, replace his HOS with Samantha's.

Obviously, the important part is for him (and you in the future) to know what that HOS stands for. He already knew that Samantha stood for Happiness. Whatever Samantha did, was driven by her HOS of Happiness. She needed to make herself happy. Many of the issues she had with Derek were because his HOS would be in direct conflict with hers. He would not be serving her HOS.

As soon as Derek decided to replace his HOS with her Happiness, things started to dramatically change. This can often happen within a day!

He would make decisions based on pleasing her HOS and not his. He would act or not act in a way that was a positive interaction with her HOS.

It was like magic and overnight, things changed. At first Samantha was puzzled and suspicious as to what was going on. However Derek persisted and soon their relationship was the strongest it had ever been.

Sure, it's not an easy thing to do. Why would you want to sacrifice your own happiness or "ways" to please someone else? You may not!
But if you do want a better interpersonal relationship with anyone, all you have to do is replace your HOS with their HOS in the times you are interacting with them. As simple as that.

OK, not so simple because it will have to be a continuous thing as long as you want a better relationship with them. As soon as you go back to your own HOS whilst interacting with them, chances are you will eventually slip back to your own ways and the relationship will be back to how it was.

The task of taking on someone's HOS is a mammoth one. No one is saying it is easy. It is literally going against yourself and everything you are and everything that drives you and makes you happy.

The question to ask is how much you want a particular human interaction to work. Maybe you won't care about taking on someone's HOS if they have bumped into you in an airport and you are getting into an argument and you want to sort it quickly!

On the other hand, you most certainly may want to take your wife or your child's HOS on board to replace yours to be able to have a better relationship with them.

It is a case of horses for courses. No one can tell you what to do in this case. However, with the knowledge from this book, you can now choose to be a much more powerful person for yourself with yourself and also in your interactions with everyone. The world is your oyster.

Taking on a person's HOS vs Adapting a new one for yourself whilst dealing with them. How do you decide?

This is important. Whether you take own someone's HOS whilst dealing with them very much depends on their HOS. For example, if someone's HOS is Religion, you can easily take this on as yourself and be more religious whilst dealing with them and have the HOS Religion running many of your systems.

Other Human Operating Systems that can easily be mimicked are for example: Kind, Humble, Thankful. The nice ones and the easy to understand ones. The ones that are "open" and non confrontational and not too complicated.

In dealing with your child, who is kind, you can easily take on their "Kind" HOS.

The ones you don't want to adapt as your own are the "bad" ones or the problematic ones. That would be silly. If someone is running on HOS "Aggressive", then you probably won't get very far along with them if you also adapted Aggressive. You may also not get far along with "Passive" if one of their subsystems is Cunning or Manipulative.

As you would expect the business of dealing with someone else and having better interpersonal relationships is not an easy one or straightforward as much as we try to make it.

80% of the cases, adapting their HOS is suitable to get you what you want. For the other 20% you can adapt their HOS IF it is an open and positive HOS.

If they are running on a negative HOS such as Rude, Manipulative or Jealous, then you have a choice. You can choose a defeating HOS or you can use NLP techniques to deal with them.

You can choose a defeating HOS by seeing what will give you the results you want.

For example, if the person is running on HOS Rude, you can run on Passive. If they are running on HOS Guilty, you can run on Gracious.

Perhaps an easier way is to use NLP in this instance:

1. Rapport Building

- **Mirroring and Matching:** Subtly mirror their body language, tone, and pace of speech to create a sense of connection and understanding.
- **Pacing and Leading:** Start by matching their emotional state (pacing) and then gradually lead them to a more positive state.

2. Reframing

- **Context Reframing:** Change the context in which the behaviour is viewed. For example, see aggressiveness as a form of passion that needs redirection.

- **Content Reframing:** Change the meaning of the behaviour. For example, interpret jealousy as a sign of admiration or desire for improvement.

3. Anchoring

- **Positive Anchoring:** Associate positive states with certain triggers (touch, word, or gesture) that can be used to shift the person's state when needed.
- **Collapsing Anchors:** Introduce a positive anchor to neutralise the negative state by triggering both simultaneously until the positive state prevails.

4. Pattern Interrupts

- **Behavioural Interrupts:** Use unexpected actions or statements to break the negative pattern. This can disrupt the negative state and create an opening for a positive interaction.
- **Linguistic Interrupts:** Ask unusual questions or make unexpected comments that shift their focus and interrupt the negative thought pattern.

5. Language Patterns

- **Milton Model:** Use indirect suggestions and ambiguous language to lead them towards a more positive mindset without triggering resistance.
- **Meta Model:** Challenge and clarify their negative statements by asking specific questions to uncover underlying beliefs and assumptions.

6. Submodalities

- **Shifting Submodalities:** Change the way they internally represent negative experiences (e.g., altering visual, auditory, or kinesthetic submodalities) to make the experiences less intense or more positive.

7. Ecology Check

- Ensure that any change aligns with their broader goals and values, and that it is sustainable and beneficial in the long term.

Example Strategy:

Dealing with Aggressiveness Using Rapport Building and Reframing

1. **Rapport Building:** Begin by matching their tone and pace to build rapport.
2. **Reframing:** Suggest that their aggressiveness is a sign of their passion and care about the issue, and propose ways to channel this passion constructively.
3. **Pattern Interrupt:** Introduce an unexpected compliment or question to break the aggressive state.
4. **Positive Anchoring:** Use a positive trigger (e.g., a calming word or gesture) when they start to show signs of calming down, reinforcing the positive state.

By employing these NLP techniques, you can adapt your interaction strategies to better handle individuals exhibiting negative behaviours, ultimately fostering more positive and constructive communication.

If they are running a HOS detrimental to you, you can use NLP to change the impact of their HOS.

4.
WHAT OUTSIDE FACTORS CAN HELP YOU CHANGE YOUR HUMAN OPERATING SYSTEM

Changing your Human Operating System is no easy feat, as mentioned several times already. This has probably been proven to you from everything you have just read.

For most people, their own mind may not be enough to make such a big decision and to stick to it. Of course, it is always preferable to make changes yourself, within yourself, by yourself and in your own mind. Circumstances help. The last straw helps. Something accidental and unexpected helps.

Other than that, it starts with the decision, the goal-setting and the persistence. However most people are not that strong and may need additional help.

You may read some of the below and think you don't have the time, budget or inclination to do any of them. That is fine. They are just there as ideas to help you.

By all means, once you have become aware of your SHOS, you can try and go it alone and make the relevant changes yourself. Keep at it and you will get there in some way.

The story of Hassan comes to mind. He was a powerful land owner in Giroft, Iran. He was ruthless, selfish, proud and impossible to deal with.
When he turned 50, he suddenly decided to change. That's how people saw it anyway. He changed.

The fact is, he changed his Human Operating System from Ruthless to Relaxed. As to the why, no one will ever know because Hassan died many years ago. However, the change was monumental and noticeable by people from all the villages around where he had his base.

Relaxed was a whole new Human Operating System and began to affect every aspect of his life as well as those around him i.e. interactions he had with others.

This chapter, we will look at some things that can help you in your quest to change your HOS and become more effective and successful in all areas of your life.

Bach Flower Remedies

Bach Flower Remedies are a form of alternative medicine developed by Dr. Edward Bach in the early 20th century.

These remedies are based on the idea that certain flowers have healing properties that can address emotional and psychological issues, ultimately promoting overall well-being.

They can in the long term and very subtly change your thoughts and have a direct effect on your Human Operating System.

Origins and Inventor

Edward Bach (1886-1936):

- **Background**: Dr. Bach was a British physician and homeopath who believed that emotional and mental states significantly impact physical health.
- **Development**: Disillusioned with conventional medicine, he sought to find natural remedies that could address the root causes of illness. Between 1928 and 1935, Bach identified 38 flowers that he believed could correspond to various emotional states.
- **Methodology**: Bach used two primary methods to create his remedies: the sun method and the boiling method. The sun method involves placing flowers in water and exposing them to sunlight, while the boiling method involves boiling the flowers in water.

How Bach Flower Remedies Work

Bach believed that each flower had a specific vibrational energy that could help to balance the corresponding emotional state. The remedies are taken orally, either directly or diluted in water, and can also be applied topically. They are intended to work by addressing emotional imbalances, which in turn can promote physical healing.

List of Bach Flower Remedies and Their Uses

1. **Agrimony**: For those who hide their troubles behind a cheerful facade and dislike being alone. Helps with facing emotions and accepting them.
2. **Aspen**: For vague fears and anxieties with no known cause. Promotes a sense of security and peace.
3. **Beech**: For those who are critical and intolerant of others. Encourages tolerance and understanding.
4. **Centaury**: For those who have difficulty saying no and are easily influenced. Helps to assert oneself.
5. **Cerato**: For those who lack confidence in their own decisions and constantly seek advice from others. Encourages self-trust and inner guidance.
6. **Cherry Plum**: For fears of losing control over one's thoughts or actions. Promotes calmness and rationality.
7. **Chestnut Bud**: For those who fail to learn from past experiences. Enhances the ability to learn and grow from experiences.
8. **Chicory**: For those who are overly possessive and expect others to conform to their needs. Fosters selfless love and care.
9. **Clematis**: For dreaminess, lack of interest in the present. Promotes a grounding and present-focused mindset.
10. **Crab Apple**: For those who feel unclean or ashamed of their appearance. Encourages self-acceptance and purification.
11. **Elm**: For those feeling overwhelmed by responsibility. Promotes confidence and capability.
12. **Gentian**: For discouragement and despondency after setbacks. Fosters optimism and perseverance.
13. **Gorse**: For hopelessness and despair. Encourages hope and a positive outlook.

14. **Heather**: For those who are self-centred and talkative. Promotes empathy and active listening.
15. **Holly**: For feelings of hatred, envy, and jealousy. Encourages unconditional love and compassion.
16. **Honeysuckle**: For those who live in the past. Encourages living in the present and looking forward to the future.
17. **Hornbeam**: For mental fatigue and lack of energy. Enhances vitality and enthusiasm.
18. **Impatiens**: For impatience and irritability. Promotes patience and calmness.
19. **Larch**: For lack of confidence and self-esteem. Encourages self-confidence and trust in one's abilities.
20. **Mimulus**: For specific known fears, such as fear of spiders, flying, or public speaking. Promotes courage and confidence.
21. **Mustard**: For deep gloom and depression with no known cause. Encourages a return to joy and lightness.
22. **Oak**: For those who never give up despite difficulties and exhaustion. Promotes balance and self-care.
23. **Olive**: For physical and mental exhaustion. Encourages restoration and renewal of energy.
24. **Pine**: For guilt and self-reproach. Encourages self-forgiveness and acceptance.
25. **Red Chestnut**: For excessive worry about the well-being of others. Promotes calmness and trust.
26. **Rock Rose**: For terror and extreme fear, often associated with panic attacks. Promotes courage and presence of mind.
27. **Rock Water**: For those who are rigid and inflexible with themselves. Encourages flexibility and relaxation.
28. **Scleranthus**: For indecision and uncertainty between two choices. Promotes decisiveness and inner certainty.
29. **Star of Bethlehem**: For shock and trauma. Promotes comfort and consolation.

30. **Sweet Chestnut**: For extreme mental anguish, feeling of despair. Encourages faith and inner peace.
31. **Vervain**: For over-enthusiasm and stress. Promotes relaxation and tolerance.
32. **Vine**: For those who are domineering and inflexible. Encourages humility and cooperation.
33. **Walnut**: For protection from change and outside influences. Promotes adaptability and protection.
34. **Water Violet**: For those who are proud, aloof, and prefer solitude. Encourages social connection and warmth.
35. **White Chestnut**: For unwanted thoughts and mental arguments. Promotes peace of mind and clarity.
36. **Wild Oat**: For uncertainty about one's direction in life. Encourages clarity and direction.
37. **Wild Rose**: For apathy and resignation. Promotes enthusiasm and active participation in life.
38. **Willow**: For resentment and self-pity. Encourages forgiveness and positivity.

Bach Flower Remedies offer a holistic approach to emotional well-being, leveraging the healing properties of flowers to address a wide range of psychological and emotional issues. These remedies focus on balancing emotional states, which can in turn promote physical health. By understanding and utilising these remedies, individuals can achieve greater emotional balance, resilience, and overall wellness. More importantly, you can change your Human Operating System by using them.

This is not going to be an overnight thing and they do take time to work and their effect is very subtle. However, they do help in changing your HOS. Read more about them online and choose up to 5 to take daily.

You can order Bach Flower Remedies from the Internet or get them from any health food store. You can put a few drops under your tongue daily or mix them in a water bottle.

Cognitive Behavioural Therapy

Bach Flower Remedies are at the top of the list to help change your Human Operating System. However, something else more useful for many to change their HOS is Cognitive Behavioural Therapy.

Cognitive Behavioural Therapy (CBT) is a widely used form of psychotherapy that focuses on identifying and modifying negative thought patterns and behaviours. It aims to improve emotional regulation and develop personal coping strategies that target solving current problems. CBT is based on the concept that thoughts, feelings, and behaviours are interconnected and that changing negative thoughts and maladaptive behaviours can lead to changes in feelings and overall well-being.

Origins of CBT

CBT was developed in the 1960s by Dr. Aaron T. Beck, a psychiatrist who noticed that his patients' negative thought patterns contributed to their emotional distress. Beck's work was influenced by earlier behavioural therapies but integrated cognitive elements to address how thoughts impact emotions and behaviour. His pioneering research led to the development of CBT as a structured, short-term, goal-oriented therapy.

How Does CBT Work?

CBT works through several key processes:

1. **Identifying Negative Thought Patterns:**
    - Clients learn to recognise and challenge distorted or unhelpful thoughts, such as overgeneralisation, catastrophising, and black-and-white thinking.

2. **Behavioural Activation:**
    - Encourages engagement in activities that are likely to improve mood and reduce avoidance behaviours.

3. **Cognitive Restructuring:**
    - Involves examining and altering negative beliefs and thoughts. Clients are taught to question the evidence for and against their thoughts and to develop more balanced perspectives.

4. **Exposure Therapy:**
    - Gradual exposure to feared situations or objects to reduce anxiety and avoidance behaviours.

5. **Skills Training:**
    - Developing practical skills such as problem-solving, stress management, and assertiveness.

6. **Homework Assignments**:
    - Clients are often given assignments to practice skills and techniques learned in therapy in real-world situations.

Effectiveness of CBT

CBT is one of the most extensively researched forms of psychotherapy, and numerous studies have demonstrated its effectiveness for a wide range of mental health issues, including:

- **Depression**: CBT helps individuals change negative thinking patterns and behaviours that contribute to their depression.
- **Anxiety Disorders**: Effective for generalised anxiety disorder, social anxiety disorder, panic disorder, and specific phobias.
- **Post-Traumatic Stress Disorder (PTSD)**: Helps individuals process and reduce distressing memories and thoughts related to trauma.
- **Obsessive-Compulsive Disorder (OCD)**: Reduces compulsions and obsessive thoughts.
- **Eating Disorders**: Addresses unhealthy eating behaviours and body image issues.
- **Substance Abuse**: Helps identify and change patterns that contribute to addiction.

How to Find a Good CBT Therapist

1. **Credentials and Training**:
    - Look for therapists who are licensed and have specific training in CBT. Common credentials include LCSW (Licensed Clinical Social Worker), LPC (Licensed Professional Counsellor), LMFT

(Licensed Marriage and Family Therapist), or Psychologist (PhD or PsyD).

2. **Experience**:
    - Check the therapist's experience with CBT and their specialisation in treating specific issues that you are facing.

3. **Referrals and Recommendations**:
    - Ask for recommendations from your primary care physician, friends, or family. You can also check with local mental health organisations.

4. **Professional Directories**:
    - Use directories from reputable organisations such as the Association for Behavioural and Cognitive Therapies (ABCT) or the American Psychological Association (APA) to find qualified therapists.

5. **Initial Consultation**:
    - Schedule a consultation to discuss your concerns and see if you feel comfortable with the therapist. This is also a chance to ask about their approach to CBT and their experience with your specific issues.

6. **Reviews and Testimonials**:
    - Look for reviews or testimonials from previous clients to gauge the therapist's effectiveness and approach.

Cognitive Behavioural Therapy is a highly effective treatment for a range of mental health issues, grounded in the idea that changing negative thought patterns and behaviours can lead to significant improvements in emotional well-being. It originated from the work of Dr. Aaron T. Beck in the 1960s and has since become one of the most researched and validated forms of psychotherapy. Finding a good CBT therapist involves looking for proper credentials, experience, and a comfortable rapport, ensuring the best outcomes for therapy.

CBT is not suitable for changing all Human Operating Systems. Just as Bach Flowers are not suited to all. However some HOS can be helped greatly with CBT.

Below is a list of things CBT can help with. You will notice some of them are Human Operating Systems. Others, whilst not on the list of general HOS, can actually be the HOS for some people, such as Schizophrenia. This can very much be someone's Human Operating System, though rare and hence not mentioned in the original list in chapter one. But do remember that illness can very much be a Human Operating System.

Here is the list of what CBT can help with:

Depression

Anxiety

OCD

PTSD

Phobias

Panic

Insomnia

- Addiction
- Bipolar
- Anger
- Aggression
- Stress
- Bulimia
- Anorexia
- Chronic pain
- ADHD
- Schizophrenia
- Social Anxiety
- Health Anxiety
- Grief
- Self-Esteem
- Guilt
- Shame
- Hopelessness
- Perfectionism
- Compulsiveness
- Self-Harm
- Suicidality

Irritability

Procrastination

Relationship Issues

Fear

Trauma

Loneliness

Isolation

Pessimism

Intrusiveness

Self-Doubt

Obsessiveness

Body Dysmorphia

Neuro-Linguistic Programming (NLP)

NLP has many tricks up it's sleeve to help with your HOS replacement. It is not within the scope of this book to cover NLP as that is a totally different method and has its own principles and beliefs.

However, some NLP principles can certainly be more beneficial than others in helping you replace your Human Operating System.

Neuro-Linguistic Programming (NLP) offers a range of tools and techniques designed to help individuals change their "human operating system" — essentially their patterns of thinking, feeling, and behaving. We touched on some of these already, here are some more of the most powerful NLP tools and how they can be applied for such transformative change:

1. Anchoring

Why: Anchoring is a technique that allows individuals to associate a particular physical or mental state with a specific trigger (like a gesture, word, or sound). This can be used to quickly shift from unresourceful states (e.g., anxiety) to resourceful states (e.g., confidence).

How: To implement anchoring, one identifies a state they want to access, fully experiences that state, and then consistently pairs it with a unique trigger. Over time, the trigger alone can elicit the desired state. For example, a person might anchor a state of calm by pressing their thumb and forefinger together while deeply relaxed.

2. Reframing

Why: Reframing involves changing the way a situation, behaviour, or thought is perceived, thereby altering its meaning and impact. This can help shift limiting beliefs and negative thought patterns.

How: To reframe a belief, one examines the context or content of the thought and finds a new perspective that is more empowering. For instance, instead of viewing a mistake as a failure, one might reframe it as a valuable learning experience.

3. Swish Pattern

Why: The Swish Pattern is designed to replace unwanted habits or responses with more desirable ones by visualising and mentally rehearsing the new behaviour.

How: One visualises the undesired behaviour and then quickly "swishes" it with a vivid image of the desired behaviour. Repeating this process builds a strong mental association, making the new behaviour more automatic.

4. Submodalities

Why: Submodalities are the finer distinctions of our sensory experiences (such as brightness, size, and location in our visual field). By altering these, one can change how they feel about certain memories or experiences.

How: Identify the submodalities of a negative experience and then change these characteristics to match those of a neutral or positive experience. For example, making a troubling image smaller and dimmer can reduce its emotional impact.

5. Meta-Model

Why: The Meta-Model is a linguistic tool used to challenge and clarify language patterns that limit thinking. It helps uncover deeper meanings and assumptions behind words.
How: By asking specific questions to clarify vague statements, uncover distortions, and challenge generalisations, one can gain deeper insight and break free from limiting beliefs. For instance, questioning statements like "I can never do anything right" helps reveal the underlying assumptions and opens up new possibilities for thinking.

6. Timeline Therapy

Why: Timeline Therapy involves working with an individual's internal timeline to heal past traumas, release negative emotions, and reprogram limiting decisions.

How: By guiding the individual to mentally revisit and reprocess significant past events from a detached perspective, they can change their emotional response and integrate more empowering beliefs about themselves and their capabilities.

7. Parts Integration

Why: Parts Integration helps resolve internal conflicts where different parts of oneself are in opposition, creating inner harmony and aligning intentions.

How: By dialoguing with the conflicting parts and finding common positive intentions behind each part's behaviour, one can integrate these parts into a cohesive whole, leading to more congruent and effective behaviour.

Practical Application for Changing the Human Operating System:

1. **Identify the Current State:** Assess the current "operating system" by identifying limiting beliefs, unwanted behaviours, and negative emotional states.
2. **Set Desired Outcomes:** Clearly define the new, beneficial "operating system" including the desired beliefs, behaviours, and emotional states.
3. **Apply NLP Techniques:**
    - Use **anchoring** to create quick access to positive states.
    - Apply **reframing** to shift perceptions of challenges and setbacks.

- Utilise the **Swish Pattern** to replace unwanted habits with constructive ones.
- Modify **submodalities** to change the emotional impact of experiences.
- Use the **Meta-Model** to challenge limiting language patterns and beliefs.
- Employ **Timeline Therapy** to heal past traumas and release negative emotions.
- Conduct **Parts Integration** to resolve internal conflicts and align intentions.

NLP, CBT and Bach Flower Remedies are each very powerful in their own way and the main recommendations of this book. There are many other ways to coax yourself to replace your HOS. Below is a list of other ways, which bear in mind, is not exhaustive and they only work for some Human Operating Systems (and their replacement):

Meditation and Mindfulness
Meditation involves practices that focus the mind and encourage heightened awareness and concentration. Mindfulness, a form of meditation, emphasises being present in the moment without judgment. These practices can reduce stress, increase emotional regulation, and promote a sense of calm and clarity, leading to profound changes in how one perceives and interacts with the world.

Hypnotherapy
Hypnotherapy uses guided relaxation and focused attention to achieve a heightened state of awareness, or trance. In this state, individuals can explore thoughts, feelings, and memories that might be hidden from their conscious mind. Hypnotherapy can help change negative thought patterns, reduce anxiety, and address various psychological issues by accessing the subconscious mind.

Positive Psychology
Positive psychology focuses on strengths, virtues, and factors that contribute to a fulfilling life. It encourages practices that foster positive emotions, engagement, relationships, meaning, and accomplishments. By emphasising what is right with individuals rather than what is wrong, positive psychology helps shift focus toward personal growth and well-being.

Emotional Freedom Techniques (EFT)
EFT, also known as tapping, combines cognitive therapy with acupressure by tapping on specific meridian points on the body while focusing on emotional issues. This technique can help release emotional blockages, reduce stress, and alleviate psychological symptoms, leading to a more balanced emotional state.

Cognitive Restructuring
Cognitive restructuring involves identifying and challenging distorted or irrational thoughts and replacing them with more accurate and positive ones. This technique, often used in cognitive-behavioural therapy, helps individuals change negative thinking patterns, which can lead to improved emotional well-being and healthier behaviours.

Visualisation and Guided Imagery
Visualisation involves creating mental images to achieve a particular goal, while guided imagery is a more structured form where someone guides you through specific visualisations. These techniques can reduce anxiety, improve performance, and promote relaxation by harnessing the power of the mind to influence physical and emotional states.

Affirmations and Positive Thinking
Affirmations are positive statements repeated regularly to challenge and overcome self-sabotaging and negative thoughts. Over time, affirmations can reprogram the mind, leading to improved self-esteem, reduced stress, and a more positive outlook on life.

Journaling and Reflective Writing
Journaling involves writing about thoughts, feelings, and experiences to gain insight and process emotions. Reflective writing encourages deeper thinking about personal experiences and lessons learned. Both practices can enhance self-awareness, clarify thoughts, and promote emotional healing.

Art Therapy
Art therapy uses creative processes like drawing, painting, and sculpting to explore emotions and experiences. It can help individuals express feelings they might find difficult to verbalise, leading to greater self-understanding, emotional release, and psychological resilience.

Music Therapy
Music therapy involves using music to address emotional, cognitive, and social needs. It can include listening to music, creating music, singing, and moving to music. Music therapy can reduce stress, improve mood, and enhance cognitive functioning by engaging different areas of the brain and promoting emotional expression.

Biofeedback and Neurofeedback
Biofeedback uses electronic monitoring to convey information about physiological processes, allowing individuals to gain control over them. Neurofeedback, a type of biofeedback, focuses on brainwave activity. These techniques can help manage stress, improve mental clarity, and treat various psychological conditions by teaching self-regulation.

Yoga and Breathwork
Yoga combines physical postures, breath control, and meditation to enhance physical and mental well-being. Breathwork focuses on controlling the breath to influence the body and mind. These practices can reduce stress, increase mindfulness, and improve emotional balance by promoting relaxation and enhancing body-mind connection.

Therapeutic Touch and Reiki
Therapeutic touch and Reiki involve energy healing practices where practitioners use their hands to balance the body's energy fields. These techniques can promote relaxation, reduce pain, and enhance overall well-being by influencing the body's natural healing processes.

Psychodynamic Therapy
Psychodynamic therapy explores unconscious processes and unresolved conflicts from the past that influence current behaviour. By bringing these issues to consciousness, individuals can gain insight and resolve inner conflicts, leading to improved mental health and personal growth.

Interpersonal Therapy (IPT)
IPT focuses on improving interpersonal relationships and social functioning to alleviate psychological symptoms. It addresses issues like unresolved grief, role transitions, and interpersonal disputes. By enhancing communication skills and resolving relational issues, IPT can improve emotional well-being.

Acceptance and Commitment Therapy (ACT)
ACT encourages individuals to accept their thoughts and feelings rather than fighting them while committing to actions aligned with their values. This approach can reduce psychological suffering and enhance life satisfaction by promoting psychological flexibility and value-driven behaviour.

Dialectical Behaviour Therapy (DBT)
DBT combines cognitive-behavioural techniques with mindfulness practices to help individuals regulate emotions, improve interpersonal relationships, and cope with distress. It is particularly effective for those with borderline personality disorder and other conditions involving emotional dysregulation.

Ayurveda and Traditional Chinese Medicine
Ayurveda and Traditional Chinese Medicine (TCM) are ancient holistic healing systems that emphasise balance in body, mind, and spirit. They use techniques such as herbal medicine, acupuncture, and dietary changes to promote health and well-being. These practices can improve mental clarity, reduce stress, and enhance overall health by restoring balance and harmony.

Gratitude Practices
Gratitude practices involve regularly focusing on and appreciating the positive aspects of life. Keeping a gratitude journal or expressing thanks can increase positive emotions, reduce stress, and enhance overall well-being by shifting focus away from negativity and fostering a more positive outlook.

Psychological Acupuncture (EFT Tapping)
Psychological acupuncture, also known as EFT tapping, combines elements of traditional acupuncture with psychological techniques. By tapping on specific meridian points while focusing on emotional issues, this method can release emotional blockages and promote psychological healing, leading to improved emotional well-being.

Use whatever works for you to get your desired results and achieve your goals. There is no right or wrong. One thing may work for someone and it may not work for another.

For example, for someone running on HOS "Stress" a simple self-talk phrase like "I am safe, there is no danger" can do wonders. For someone else running on Stress, it can do nothing - whereas Meditation can do wonders for them.

5.
CONCLUSION

Human Psychology has evolved over the centuries. Let's highlight a summary:

Ancient Practices

1. **Meditation and Mindfulness (circa 5000 BCE)**
    - **Origins:** Ancient India and China.
    - **Method:** Techniques like meditation, practiced in Hinduism, Buddhism, and Taoism, focused on mindfulness and self-awareness.
    - **Purpose:** To achieve mental clarity, reduce stress, and enhance spiritual growth.

2. **Stoicism (3rd century BCE)**

- **Key Figures:** Zeno of Citium, Seneca, Epictetus, Marcus Aurelius.
- **Method:** Emphasising rationality and self-control to overcome destructive emotions.
- **Purpose:** To attain inner peace and resilience by aligning with nature and focusing on what can be controlled.

Early Modern Era

3. **Psychoanalysis (Late 19th - Early 20th Century)**
   - **Key Figure:** Sigmund Freud.
   - **Method:** Exploring the unconscious mind through techniques like free association and dream analysis.
   - **Purpose:** To uncover repressed emotions and experiences that influence behaviour, leading to self-awareness and healing.

4. **Behaviourism (Early 20th Century)**
   - **Key Figures:** John B. Watson, B.F. Skinner.
   - **Method:** Using reinforcement and punishment to shape behaviour through conditioning.
   - **Purpose:** To modify behaviours by understanding and changing environmental influences.

Mid to Late 20th Century

5. **Humanistic Psychology (1950s-1960s)**
   - **Key Figures:** Carl Rogers, Abraham Maslow.
   - **Method:** Emphasising self-actualisation and personal growth through client-centred therapy and the hierarchy of needs.

- **Purpose:** To help individuals achieve their full potential and improve self-esteem by focusing on their inherent goodness and personal experiences.

6. **Cognitive Behavioural Therapy (CBT) (1960s)**

    - **Key Figures:** Aaron T. Beck, Albert Ellis.
    - **Method:** Combining cognitive and behavioural techniques to change negative thought patterns and behaviours.
    - **Purpose:** To treat various psychological disorders and improve mental health by addressing distorted thinking and fostering positive behaviour changes.

7. **Neuro-Linguistic Programming (NLP) (1970s)**

    - **Key Figures:** Richard Bandler, John Grinder.
    - **Method:** Analysing and replicating successful behaviours and thought patterns through language and neurological processes.
    - **Purpose:** To enhance personal development and communication skills by modelling effective strategies.

Contemporary Methods

8. **Mindfulness-Based Cognitive Therapy (MBCT) (1990s)**

    - **Key Figures:** Zindel Segal, Mark Williams, John Teasdale.
    - **Method:** Integrating mindfulness practices with cognitive therapy techniques.
    - **Purpose:** To prevent relapse in depression and reduce stress by increasing present-moment awareness and acceptance.

9. **Positive Psychology (Late 20th - Early 21st Century)**
   - **Key Figures:** Martin Seligman, Mihaly Csikszentmihalyi.
   - **Method:** Focusing on strengths, virtues, and factors that contribute to a fulfilling life.
   - **Purpose:** To promote well-being and happiness by emphasising positive experiences and attributes.

10. **Acceptance and Commitment Therapy (ACT) (1980s)**
    - **Key Figure:** Steven C. Hayes.
    - **Method:** Using acceptance and mindfulness strategies mixed with commitment and behaviour-change strategies.
    - **Purpose:** To increase psychological flexibility by helping individuals accept their thoughts and feelings and commit to actions aligned with their values.

11. **Dialectical Behaviour Therapy (DBT) (1990s)**
    - **Key Figure:** Marsha M. Linehan.
    - **Method:** Combining cognitive-behavioural techniques with mindfulness practices.
    - **Purpose:** To treat borderline personality disorder and other conditions by balancing acceptance and change.

Modern Integrative Approaches

12. **Integrative and Holistic Therapies (21st Century)**
    - **Method:** Combining elements from various psychological theories and practices, such as

    cognitive-behavioural, humanistic, and psychodynamic approaches.
  - **Purpose:** To provide a comprehensive treatment that addresses multiple aspects of a person's mental health and well-being.

The evolution of psychological methods for self-improvement reflects humanity's ongoing quest for understanding and enhancing the mind. From ancient practices of meditation and Stoicism to contemporary approaches like CBT, NLP, and mindfulness-based therapies, each method offers unique insights and tools for personal growth and mental well-being. These methods continue to evolve, integrating new research and techniques to address the complexities of human psychology.

Nothing worth doing is going to be easy. It is by going through hardships and challenges that we grow. It is perhaps sad and harsh but such is the reality of life.

A smooth sea, never made a skilled sailor.

The Secret Human Operating System is a novel idea in many ways. Other practitioners or human development leaders perhaps have other names for it; or no name for it!

Many will not accept the simple fact that there is ONE main operating system for each human at different times of their life. To them, the human being is far too complex to be commandeered by just one idea, one drive, one system.

As we have seen in this book, this is perhaps true for many, in that they will have one Human Operating System and several subsystems sitting closely under it and all acting together.

However, the simple fact remains that it is only the one Human Operating System that is the dominant driving force in your life.

The undeniable proof lies in the transformative impact of uncovering this Human Operating System (HOS). Once revealed, it unlocks immense potential for personal development and growth, profoundly enhancing not only one's self-awareness and capabilities but also enriching relationships with others. Discovering your HOS is the key to achieving extraordinary results and realising your full potential.

Now that you have come this far, have faith and try the principles in this book. You have nothing to lose and everything to gain. You will view the world differently and you will achieve so much more.

However, the caveat with the Human Operating System as with most things requiring determination is the effort needed and the perseverance.

Even if you achieve results and go back to your old ways, like most people, you will have the confidence knowing that you can always come back and pick up this book and start the transformation all over again. It will work every time as long as you are patient and persistent.

The very best of luck to you.

www.ingramcontent.com/pod-product-compliance
Lightning Source LLC
Chambersburg PA
CBHW071837210526
45479CB00001B/170